GREAT BIBLE TRIVIA FOR KIDS

Tamela Hancock Murray

BARBOUR
PUBLISHING

© 2000 by Barbour Publishing, Inc.

ISBN 1-57748-655-2

All rights reserved. No part of this publication may be reproduced or transmitted in any form or by any means without written permission of the publisher.

Scripture marked KJV is taken from the King James Version of the Bible.

Scripture marked NIV is taken from the HOLY BIBLE: NEW INTERNATIONAL VERSION ®. NIV ®. Copyright © 1973, 1978, 1984 by International Bible Society. Used by permission of Zondervan Publishing House. All rights reserved.

Published by Barbour Publishing, Inc., P.O. Box 719, Uhrichsville, Ohio 44683, www.barbourbooks.com

Illustrations © Ron Wheeler www.cartoonworks.com

ԑсpа Member of the
Evangelical Christian
Publishers Association

Printed in the United States of America.
5 4

GREAT BIBLE TRIVIA
FOR KIDS

THE OLD TESTAMENT

1) True or false: Most of the Old Testament was originally written in the Hebrew language.

2) True or false: The Old Testament was written before Christ was born.

3) The first five books of the Bible are called the:
   a) Pentateuch.
   b) Pentagon.
   c) Pentimento.
   d) Fantastic Five.

4) Who wrote the first five books of the Bible?

5) Did you know the Jewish people call the first five books of the Bible the Torah? These books contain the Law given to Moses by God. Today, many Jewish people follow dietary laws and other observances set forth in the Torah. Jesus said Christians do not need to follow these laws. (John 1:17) However, we worship the same God, Jehovah, and Christians are to follow the Ten Commandments.

6) You can find the Ten Commandments in the following Old Testament book(s):
   a) Exodus.
   b) Deuteronomy.
   c) Exodus and Deuteronomy.
   d) Genesis.

7) Can you name all of the Ten Commandments?

8) The first event in the Old Testament is the:
   a) creation of the universe.
   b) creation of the first gospel singing group.
   c) great flood.
   d) birth of Jesus.

9) In the Old Testament, the nation of Israel was divided into how many tribes?

10) What are the names of the twelve tribes of Israel?

11) The Law in the Pentateuch is often called the Mosaic Law because:
a) God gave the laws to Moses.
b) all the laws are different, creating a "mosaic" of instructions.
c) Moses broke the stone tablets and made up his own law.
d) Moses was a police officer.

12) Why do you think there are so many names listed in several of the early Old Testament books?

13) The Book of Ruth:
   a) is named for the candy bar, Baby Ruth.
   b) records great military victories.
   c) is the story of an evil woman named Ruth.
   d) illustrates two kinds of love.

14) Esther:
   a) held a triathlon to see who would be her king.
   b) won a beauty contest and married the king.
   c) paid the king a lot of money to marry her because she was ugly.
   d) was not Jewish.

15) True or false: Queen Esther is honored by Jewish people today.

16) The Book of Job relates how:
   a) to get a good job.
   b) God protects and rewards those who love Him.
   c) to cover up those ugly sores.
   d) friends help out when the going gets tough.

17) True or false: King David, who wrote many of the Psalms, was the father of King Solomon, who wrote Ecclesiastes and most of Proverbs.

18) A psalter:
   a) sprinkles salt.
   b) mines salt.
   c) makes a habit of asking, "Would you please pass the salt?"
   d) sings praises to God.

19) Did you know the word psalm means religious song? The Book of Psalms is a collection of worshipful songs praising the Lord. Although David wrote many of them, others contributed to this book as well. Psalms from this book are often used in church worship services. You might also use them as prayers when you talk to God by yourself. Take a look at the Book of Psalms. See if you can find one that speaks to you today.

20) Anyone looking for wisdom from King Solomon can consult:
   a) *Sports Illustrated.*
   b) John.
   c) Proverbs.
   d) Psalms.

21) True or false: King Solomon also wrote the Book of Lamentations.

22) Ecclesiastes teaches us that:
   a) earth's glories fade, but God is forever.
   b) Solomon should have picked an easier title
      to spell than Ecclesiastes.
   c) Solomon had very little money.
   d) Solomon had trouble in school.

23) True or false: We know
    who wrote all of the
    books of the Old
    Testament.

24) Pretend you are a Bible scholar trying to find out when the events of a certain book of the Bible took place. What would you look for?

25) A prophet is:
   a) an astronomer.
   b) a psychic.
   c) one who interprets dreams.
   d) one sent by God to tell His plans for the future.

26) A true prophet:
   a) always has good news.
   b) is not always sent from God.
   c) works for profit.
   d) often is sent to warn God's people to repent of sin.

27) The Old Testament includes the prophecies of both major and minor prophets. The words of major prophets can be found in Isaiah, Jeremiah, Lamentations, Ezekiel, and Daniel. The

prophecies of twelve minor prophets follow. Each book is named after the prophet who wrote it, with the exception of Lamentations. The Lamentations are poems of sadness.

28) Jonah was swallowed by:
   a) debt.
   b) the mechanical fish from the movie *Jaws*.
   c) a big fish.
   d) a one-eyed, one-horned, flying purple people eater.

BREAD

1) True or false: Bread is not mentioned in the Bible until the New Testament.

2) People in Bible times sometimes baked bread without yeast because they were in a hurry. Bread without yeast is faster to prepare than bread using yeast. This is because yeast takes an hour or so to rise, during which time the dough doubles in size. Some recipes call for letting the dough rise twice, so baking might take all afternoon.

3) Esau sold his birthright to his brother Jacob for bread and:
   a) a letter promising a $10 million sweepstakes prize.
   b) a bowl of lentil stew.
   c) a cup of water.
   d) a pat of butter.

4) What did Esau also sell when he sold his birthright?

5) Here's how bread played a role when Jacob stole Esau's birthright. Isaac, Esau and Jacob's father, asked Esau for food before he gave him his blessing. (Genesis 27:4)

6) True or false: Esau and Jacob's mother, Rebekah, helped Jacob trick Isaac into giving Jacob the blessing that belonged to Esau.

7) Jacob was able to trick Isaac because Isaac was:
    a) old and blind.
    b) dull-witted.
    c) stuck up.
    d) too busy watching the NBA playoffs.

8) Were Esau and Jacob identical twins, meaning they looked alike, or fraternal twins, meaning they did not look alike? How do we know?

9) What Old Testament book tells how God delivered His people from Egypt and led them to the wilderness?

10) While the Israelites were living in the wilderness, God provided:
    a) ginger ale and peanut butter crackers.
    b) casseroles made by Egyptian women.
    c) locusts and wild honey.
    d) manna.

11) In Proverbs 31:27, King Solomon says a good wife does not eat the bread of:
   a) Israel.
   b) idleness (laziness).
   c) ugliness.
   d) Pepperidge Farm.

12) The Book of Ecclesiastes contains mostly:
   a) history.
   b) law.
   c) movie reviews.
   d) words of wisdom.

13) Ecclesiastes 11:1 (NIV) contains a famous phrase: "Cast your bread upon the waters, for after many days you will find it again." What does that mean?

14) Ecclesiastes was written by:
   a) King Solomon.   c) Steven Spielberg.
   b) Noah.   d) Mister Rogers.

15) This same person also wrote:
   a) Proverbs.
   b) several Hardy Boys mysteries.
   c) articles for *Readers' Digest.*
   d) Jude.

16) Did you know Satan tempted Jesus to make bread out of stones? (Matthew 4:3)

17) Why was it tempting for Jesus to turn stones into bread?

18) When Satan told Jesus to turn stones into bread, Jesus answered, "It is written, Man shall not live by bread alone, but by every word that proceedeth out of the mouth of God." (Matthew 4:4, KJV) What does this mean?

19) Jesus said what He told Satan was written somewhere. To what Scripture was He referring?

20) Think about the last time you were tempted. What did you do?

21) Can you recite the Lord's Prayer?

22) What does this prayer say about bread?

23) Jesus called Himself:
   a) the manna of man.   c) the bread of life.
   b) divine.   d) the world's best teacher.

24) Today in church we remember how Jesus is the bread of life through a special sacrament. What is it called?

25) What do you do in your life to show you believe in Jesus?

NOT EXACTLY JUDGE JUDY

1) Where in the Old Testament can we find out about the judges of Israel?

2) Did you know the name Deborah means "hornet"?

3) True or false: Women judges were common in the Old Testament.

4) Deborah was also a:
   a) clerk at a video store.
   b) soccer player.
   c) computer programmer.
   d) prophet.

5) True or false: In Deborah's time, Israel was a free nation.

6) King Jabin of Canaan:
   a) made life very hard for the Israelites.
   b) promised to get rid of baseball trading cards.
   c) forced the Israelites to worship gold statues of himself.
   d) served pepperoni pizza in school cafeterias every Friday.

7) How many iron chariots did King Jabin have?

8) How many years did the Israelites live under King Jabin's rule before they asked God for help?

9) Why was God punishing Israel at this time?

10) True or false: After the people cried out for help, the Lord told Deborah what to do to deliver her people.

11) Deborah planned to:
   a) poison the enemy's water supply.
   b) pray for a plague of frogs to torture the
      enemy.
   c) deliver the enemy into the
      hands of Israel's
      general.
   d) ask the general to
      use stealth
      fighter planes
      to bomb
      the enemy.

12) The enemy was to be defeated at Mount Tabor. Where was Mount Tabor located?

13) Many scholars believe that Jesus' Transfiguration took place on Mount Tabor. At the Transfiguration Jesus was visited by Moses and Elijah. (Matthew 17:1–9; Mark 9:1–10; Luke 9:28–36)

14) Barak was:
   a) awarded a Purple Heart medal for bravery.
   b) the inventor of the nuclear submarine.
   c) a general in Israel's army.
   d) Deborah's husband.

15) Rather than confront the enemy alone, Barak wanted to take along:
   a) Deborah, to ensure success.
   b) his hand-held video game in case he got bored.
   c) his lucky rabbit's foot.
   d) 10,000 men, to outnumber the king's army.

16) Deborah agreed, but said the credit for the victory would go to:
   a) Barak.
   b) a woman.
   c) McDonald's, for providing the army with hamburgers.
   d) Pepsi, Reebok, and Tide, the army's corporate sponsors.

17) True or false: In Old Testament times, it was customary for women in Israel to lead battles because in that nation, they were considered superior to men.

18) Did God give the Israelites complete victory over Sisera's army?

19) You can read a poem about the battle in:
   a) the fifth chapter of Judges.
   b) the first chapter of Genesis.
   c) The Butter Battle Book by Dr. Seuss.
   d) the Book of Revelation.

20) After the people of Israel cried out to God for help, He answered their prayers. When was the last time you prayed to God for help? What happened?

TALKING TO GOD

1) True or false: We can pray to God anytime.

2) When we pray to God, we should first:
   a) praise Him.
   b) ask for whatever we want.
   c) ask for bad weather so school will close.
   d) tell Him we haven't done anything wrong.

3) What Old Testament book contains many songs and prayers?

4) Most of the Psalms were written by:
   a) David.   c) Moses.
   b) Adam.   d) Mary.

5) Did you know when you worship and pray with other people in your congregation, it is called corporate worship? Although praying alone is important, corporate worship is one way to take part in the Christian community.

6) True or false: In Old Testament times, people never prayed directly to God.

7) True or false: Abraham's servant asked for God's guidance when he was told to choose a wife for Isaac.

8) After Isaac married Rebekah, Isaac prayed for:
   a) a home gym so he could lose the weight he had gained from his wife's cooking.
   b) a second wife, like so many Old Testament men.
   c) permission to join the Canaanite Bowling League.
   d) Rebekah to have a baby.

9) Confession is the part of a prayer where we tell God about our sins. Although God already knows our sins, when we confess them to Him, He knows we understand we did wrong. We should ask Him to forgive us for our sins. After that, we should sincerely try not to commit those sins in the future.

10) Here is a portion of a prayer Moses prayed (Deuteronomy 9:26–27, NIV): "O Sovereign LORD, do not destroy your people, your own inheritance that you redeemed by your great power and brought out of Egypt with a mighty hand. Remember your servants Abraham, Isaac and Jacob. Overlook the stubbornness of this people, their wickedness and their sin." What word shows that Moses worships God? Can you find the sentence of confession?

11) When we go to God in prayer, we should:
   a) be humble.
   b) convince Him how great we are.
   c) give Him a list of our accomplishments in church.
   d) tell Him all about the latest *Star Wars* movie.

12) When we ask God for something, it is called a petition. Although God wants us to express our wants and needs to Him, our prayers should not be full of petitions without praise or thanksgiving. Not every prayer needs to have a petition. You can simply give thanks to God or praise Him.

13) Have you ever prayed for something and received it, and then wish you hadn't asked God for it? Think about it.

14) When the people in Samuel's time wanted a king instead of a judge, God answered their request even though He knew judges would be best. (1 Samuel 8:6–7)

15) True or false: After God allowed Israel to be ruled by kings, most of the kings proved to be good.

16) When Jonah tried to escape God's will, he:
   a) was swallowed by a big fish.
   b) proved successful in his attempt to escape.
   c) told God he would go to Nineveh if He would name a Bible book after him.
   d) wrote a book called *Jonah's Travels*.

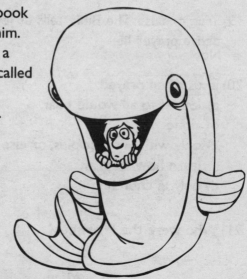

17) True or false: When Jonah was in trouble, he prayed to God.

18) Before Jesus was crucified, He prayed that God would change His mind about allowing Him to die in such a horrible way. (Matthew 26:39) Sometimes God wants us to do something we don't want to do.

19) True or false: The Bible tells us Jesus had an active prayer life.

20) Jesus often prayed:
   a) loudly, so all would hear.
   b) alone.
   c) only with His disciples, or else others would learn how to pray.
   d) only in church.

21) Who were the Pharisees?

22) The Bible tells of a Pharisee who prayed:
   a) loudly, boasting about his goodness.
   b) silently.
   c) in French, a language unheard of at that time.
   d) for God to have mercy upon him.

23) The tax collector:
   a) applauded the Pharisee for his goodness.
   b) admitted his sin and asked God for mercy.
   c) said he gave even more to the treasury than the Pharisee.
   d) asked the Pharisee how he could enroll in middle school.

24) Why were tax collectors in Jesus' day hated and considered sinful?

25) True or false: Jesus praised the Pharisee.

26) True or false: It is all right to ask God to crush our enemies.

27) Regarding enemies, Jesus said we are to:
   a) love them.   c) pray for them.
   b) bless them.   d) all of the above.

28) True or false: When you pray, you should always give thanks to God.

29) Name five things you can thank God for today.

A WICKED KING

1) Israel was divided into two kingdoms at the time Ahab ruled. After King Solomon died, the kingdom divided into Israel and Judah. Each kingdom had a separate king. At the time Ahab began his rule of Israel in Samaria, Asa was king of Judah. (1 Kings 16:29)

2) True or false: All the kings of Israel during the time of the Book of 1 Kings were good.

3) King Ahab ruled Israel from 874 to 853 B.C. This was over 800 years before Jesus was born.

4) King Ahab:
   a) loved the God of Israel.
   b) worshiped the god Baal.
   c) promised the people new high schools.
   d) sponsored free gospel music concerts in the mall.

5) Baal was the pagan god of:
   a) fertility.   c) famine.
   b) war.   d) math students.

6) King Ahab's wife was named:
   a) Mary Margaret.   c) Belle.
   b) Jezebel.   d) Cruella.

7) True or false: After King Ahab married,
   he rededicated his life to the God of Israel.

8) True or false: Ahab angered God more than
   any king of Israel before him.

9) God sent Elijah the prophet to tell Ahab there
   would be a drought until:
   a) Ahab changed his ways.
   b) Ahab sacrificed a lamb, two rams, and three
      turtledoves.
   c) God commanded it to rain.
   d) the poets run out of rhymes.

10) Did you know God allowed King Ahab's army to kill 100,000 Syrians? (1 Kings 20:29) Because the Syrians said God was a god of the mountains, they thought they could defeat Israel If a war were fought in the flat plains below. By giving Israel victory on the plains, God was showing He rules the earth.

11) True or false: God sent His prophet Elijah to tell Ahab's people not to follow Baal.

12) What is a vineyard?

13) King Ahab wanted the vineyard of Naboth the Jezreelite because:
   a) it was near his palace and he wanted to use it as a vegetable garden.
   b) it was a perfect location to film his latest movie.
   c) he needed the land so he could build a temple to Baal.
   d) his goats needed more land for pasture.

14) In return for the vineyard, King Ahab promised Naboth:
   a) a better vineyard or to pay him what it was worth.
   b) 1,000 dancing girls and a herd of goats.
   c) blessings from Baal.
   d) season tickets to see the Washington Redskins.

15) Naboth refused to let King Ahab have the vineyard because:
   a) he had lost the deed to the land in a Monopoly game.
   b) the land belonged to his mother-in-law.
   c) the land was not good enough for the glorious King Ahab.
   d) God refused to let him give King Ahab the land.

16) After Naboth refused to give Ahab the land, the king:
   a) threw his video games at the TV.
   b) stamped his feet, shook his fists, and cried.
   c) sulked and refused to eat.
   d) prayed to Baal to curse Naboth.

17) True or false: After seeing her husband's anger, Ahab's wife plotted to kill Naboth.

18) Did Ahab's wife get revenge on Naboth?

19) When Naboth's vineyard became available, King Ahab:
a) took it.
b) celebrated by playing the ukulele.
c) paid Naboth's family ten times what the land was worth.
d) sent the dancing girls and goats he had promised.

20) True or false: The God of Israel was not fooled by Jezebel's clever plan of revenge upon Naboth.

21) Who gave King Ahab the message from God that Ahab would pay for his sin?

22) True or false: Ahab's punishment from the Lord was death.

23) Even though Ahab's wife, Jezebel, put the plan of revenge into place, why do you think God still blamed and punished Ahab?

MEET ELIJAH

1) We first meet Elijah in:
   a) I Kings.
   b) Genesis.
   c) Acts.
   d) his swimming trunks.

2) Elijah was:
   a) a doctor.
   b) an actor playing the role of a doctor.
   c) a prophet.
   d) the writer of the Gospel of John.

3) Elijah was from Tishbe in Gilead. Gilead was located southeast of the Sea of Galilee. The exact location of the city of Tishbe is not known.

4) True or false: Elijah served the Lord of Israel.

5) Elijah told King Ahab there would be:
   a) great profits from his new racetrack.
   b) seven years of bounty, followed by seven years of famine.
   c) a great ship named *Titanic* that would sink on her maiden voyage.
   d) no rain for the next few years until God commanded rain to fall.

6) Why do you think God told Elijah to give King Ahab this message?

7) True or false: King Ahab was a godly king who loved the Lord.

8) King Ahab:
   a) honored the God of Israel with sacrifices pleasing to Him.
   b) worshiped the god Baal.
   c) went on television to proclaim God's greatness.
   d) was the best king Israel ever had.

9) God told Elijah to hide by Kerith Ravine. (1 Kings 17:2–3) A ravine is a gorge or gap in the land. The King James Version of the Bible calls this location brook Cherith. We can assume from this that brook Cherith was located in Kerith Ravine.

10) Kerith Ravine was located:
   a) east of Eden.   c) east of Jordan.
   b) west of Jordan.   d) near one of Michael Jordan's homes.

11) God told Elijah to hide because:
   a) Elijah's prophecy had made King Ahab mad.
   b) he was famous and God wanted him to avoid photographers.
   c) King Ahab wanted to honor him with food forbidden to Jews.
   d) hide-and-seek was the favorite game of King Ahab's small son.

12) While he was hiding, Elijah's food would be brought to him by:
   a) ravens.
   b) doves.
   c) pretty maids all in a row.
   d) an ice cream truck, since the ravine was on its route.

13) Look at your answer to the last question. Why would they bring Elijah his food?

14) Elijah's food consisted of:
   a) bagels and lox in the morning and matzo ball soup in the evening.
   b) eggs and bacon in the morning and a ham and cheese sandwich in the evening.
   c) any food his heart desired.
   d) bread and meat in the morning and evening.

15) After the brook dried up, Elijah was fed by:
   a) bigger, better ravens.   c) locusts.
   b) a widow.   d) John the Baptist.

16) Why did the brook dry up?

17) True or false: The widow who fed Elijah after the brook dried up had plenty of rich food to eat.

18) After the widow's son died, Elijah:
   a) told her she shouldn't have let him hang out on the street corner.
   b) gave her herbs and green tea.
   c) said she should have called 911 sooner.
   d) prayed to God.

19) True or false: The widow's son rose from the dead.

20) Jesus called John the Baptist "the Elijah." (Matthew 11:14, 17:12; Mark 9:13) This was great praise for the ministry and prophecies of John the Baptist and a clue that Jesus is the Messiah.

21) Some people said Jesus was:
   a) Elijah.
   b) John the Baptist.
   c) Jeremiah.
   d) all of the above.

22) True or false: Jesus spoke to Moses and Elijah before He was crucified.

23) Why would the Jews be looking for Elijah to come back from the dead?

24) True or false: Jesus said Elijah had returned.

25) You can read more about the life of Elijah in 1 Kings and 2 Kings. Elijah was God's servant. God took care of Elijah, just as He takes care of people today who belong to Him. How does God take care of you?

GOD PROVIDES FOR THE POOR

1) True or false: God did not have any special consideration for the poor until Jesus spoke about them in the New Testament.

2) Usury is:
   a) using other people's possessions without permission.
   b) charging people interest, or extra money, to borrow money.
   c) using other people's money.
   d) giving people free use of the Internet.

3) Under Old Testament law, was usury acceptable?

4) About giving people money, Jesus said:
   a) to ignore the Old Testament law entirely.
   b) people who spend too much deserve what they get.
   c) to throw those who borrowed into debtor's prison.
   d) if you make a loan, do not expect repayment.

5) True or false: God said to let poor people win lawsuits because they are poor.

6) When you glean a field, you:
   a) sell it.
   b) gather leftover crops after the harvest.
   c) use it to bury the dead.
   d) cut down all the trees on it.

7) What was the name of the poor woman who gleaned Boaz's fields? (Hint: A book of the Bible bears her name.)

8) In Bible times, people would sometimes use their clothing as security for a loan. People with nothing else to give but their clothing were the poorest of the Israelites. Since clothing took a long time to make, wearable items were not plentiful as they are today. Coats often doubled as beds. That is why God commanded that anyone who took a cloak in exchange for a loan had to return it by sundown so its owner would have a place to sleep. (Deuteronomy 24:12–13)

9) Poor people were to be paid their salaries:
   a) once a year.
   b) in French francs.
   c) in manna.
   d) before sundown at the end of each workday.

10) True or false: When King David saw the beautiful Bathsheba, he sent her husband to the front lines of a battle to be killed and took her for himself.

11) To show King David the greatness of his sin, the prophet Nathan told him a story about:
   a) a rich man and a poor man.
   b) the prodigal son.
   c) the lazy fox and the red hen.
   d) the tortoise and the hare.

12) Part of the Jewish celebration of Purim is sending gifts to the poor (Esther 9:22). This holiday was established to celebrate Esther's bravery in saving her people from death.

13) In Matthew 19:21, what did Jesus tell the rich young ruler he must do to be perfect?

14) When the rich young ruler heard Jesus' instructions, he immediately:
   a) left his home and pledged his life to mission work.
   b) built a new church.
   c) developed a line of Christian computer games.
   d) walked away sadly, for he owned much.

15) When a woman in Bethany poured expensive ointment on His head, Jesus:
   a) said she had done something good for Him.
   b) was furious that his hairstyle was mussed.
   c) thought the gesture was a waste of money.
   d) sent her the bill for having His cloak dry cleaned.

16) Did you know the ointment was worth about 300 pence? This was about one year's wages. (Mark 14:5)

17) True or false: The disciples thought the ointment should have been sold and the money given to the poor.

18) The Jewish people often gave gifts to the poor as part of the Passover celebration. Note that the ointment was poured on Jesus' head near Passover, which most likely prompted the objection.

19) Why did Jesus say that the poor widow who donated two mites to the treasury gave more than the rich people who gave a lot of money?

20) True or false: The poor are blessed because they will inherit the kingdom of God.

21) When the beggar Lazarus asked the rich man for food, the rich man:
   a) did not show him any mercy.
   b) invited him to share Thanksgiving turkey.
   c) gave him food, as well as a fine new cloak and a bed to sleep in.
   d) threw a penny at him.

22) True or false: In the afterlife, the roles of the rich man and the beggar were reversed.

23) In his first letter to the Corinthians, Paul says:
   a) giving to the poor will get you into heaven.
   b) the government should take care of the poor.
   c) "Woe is I! My ink doth runneth out, and I have ten more letters to write!"
   d) no matter how much you give to the poor, it's no good without love.

GOD'S SPECIAL DAYS

1) True or false: The Feast of Unleavened Bread was established by God.

2) Unleavened bread is made:
   a) without yeast.
   b) with yeast.
   c) in an oven that is off-balance.
   d) by the Wonder company.

3) The Feast of Unleavened Bread was celebrated to remember:
   a) not to run out of yeast.
   b) that man does not live by bread alone.
   c) how God brought the Israelites out of Egypt.
   d) that Jesus is the Messiah.

4) The Feast of Unleavened Bread was first established in what Old Testament book? (Hint: Consider what the feast commemorates.)

5) Did you know that the penalty for breaking the Feast of Unleavened Bread was severe? (Exodus 12:19)

6) How many days did the Feast of Unleavened Bread last?

7) True or false: If an Israelite were away from home, it was permissible for that person to eat leavened bread during the feast days.

8) In Old Testament times, the first month of the new year was not January but March or April. God established this calendar, which went along with the ancient harvest seasons. (Exodus 12:1–2) The first month of the year was called Abib, or Nisan. This was the time of the barley and flax harvests.

9) True or false: Another important Jewish holiday celebrated during the Feast of Unleavened Bread is Passover.

10) To punish Egypt for enslaving Israel, God sent the angel of death to take the firstborn of every Egyptian household. The Jews were to escape this punishment by marking their doors with:

a) lamb's blood.
c) Christmas lights.
b) a yellow ribbon.
d) a cross.

11) True or false: Since they left Egypt long ago, Jews today don't celebrate Passover.

12) Did you know Jesus' parents traveled to Jerusalem each year to celebrate Passover? (Luke 2:41) During one of these trips, Jesus was left behind at the temple. This is the only episode of Jesus' childhood recorded in the Bible.

13) The Feast of Unleavened Bread began:
   a) the day after Passover.
   b) the day before Passover.
   c) on Moses' birthday.
   d) when everyone ran out of yeast.

14) True or false: Jesus' enemies plotted to arrest him two days before Passover.

15) Jesus' enemies did not want him arrested during the Feast of Unleavened Bread because they:
   a) wanted Jesus to miss out on all the good food.
   b) wanted Jesus to turn water into wine for them.
   c) were afraid the Jews might riot.
   d) were afraid that would ruin their celebration.

16) True or false: When Jesus appeared before Pontius Pilate, the ruler found Jesus guilty of several crimes.

17) During Passover, it was the custom for the ruler to:
   a) renew his commitment to God.
   b) sing "Rock of Ages" at the Coliseum.
   c) throw a Christian to the lions.
   d) release one prisoner.

18) True or false: When the Jews begged Pilate to release Jesus, he refused.

19) Did you know that in areas of the United States with large Jewish populations, you will often see foods marked "kosher"? This means the food has been prepared in accordance with Jewish law and blessed by a rabbi. If you live in a big city, such as New York City, you may already be accustomed to seeing this designation. If not, try looking in your local grocery store for kosher foods a month or so before Easter, which is usually around the time of Passover. See how many you can find.

20) True or false: Today all Christians make a special effort to cook lamb on Passover to remember God.

21) The Feast of Harvest was also called the Feast of Weeks. This is because it was held seven weeks after the Feast of Unleavened Bread.

22) True or false: The Feast of Harvest celebrated the first fruits of the harvest, and the Feast of Ingathering was celebrated at the end of the year.

23) Did you know the Feast of Weeks is also called the Feast of Pentecost? That is because there were fifty days between Pentecost and an offering of bread made after Passover. The word pentecost means "fiftieth."

24) True or false: The Feast of Trumpets took place to commemorate the seventh month, which would have been September or October.

25) The Day of Atonement gave Israelites the opportunity to:
a) add toner to copy machines.
b) "tone down" red hair color resulting from too much henna.
c) catch some rays.
d) make amends for their sins.

26) True or false: Today, many Jewish people recognize the Day of Atonement.

27) The Feast of the Tabernacles commemorated:
a) Jesus' birth in a stable.
b) the building of Solomon's temple.
c) the forty years' wandering in the wilderness.
d) the Mormon Tabernacle Choir.

28) During the Feast of the Tabernacles, native Israelites were instructed to live in:
a) stables.
b) the temple.
c) booths.
d) choir lofts.

29) Since Christians worship God the Father, why don't Christians celebrate the days in this quiz?

A NEW TEMPLE

1) Did you know the name Ezra means "Jehovah Helps"?

2) True or false: The Book of Ezra mentions Ezra several times.

3) The Book of Ezra is located in:
   a) the Old Testament, just before Nehemiah.
   b) the New Testament, just before Nehemiah.
   c) the book of Jewish history written by Josephus.
   d) Lifestyles of Rich and Famous Priests.

4) The Book of Ezra opens with:
   a) Christ's birth.
   b) the end of the Jews' captivity in Babylon.
   c) a psalm of David.
   d) a prophecy about the end of the world.

5) Who decreed a new temple would be built in Jerusalem?

6) After this decree, how many people returned to the land?

7) True or false: No one opposed rebuilding God's temple.

8) True or false: The new temple would be even greater and more beautiful than the one Solomon built.

9) Artaxerxes was king of:
   a) Israel.
   c) Babylon.
   b) Persia.
   d) England.

10) Was Artaxerxes as friendly to Israel as King Cyrus?

11) Israel's enemies let King Artaxerxes know Jerusalem was being rebuilt by:
   a) blowing trumpets until Persia's walls fell down.
   b) a comedy routine delivered by a court jester.
   c) sending a letter.
   d) broadcasting a special program on television.

12) King Artaxerxes found the city of Jerusalem to be:
   a) peaceful.
   b) fun-loving.
   c) on the cutting edge of technology.
   d) rebellious.

13) Was King Artaxerxes's observation true?

14) King Artaxerxes ordered that:
   a) a festival be held each year to honor Jerusalem.
   b) everyone in Persia was to worship Jehovah.
   c) the city not be rebuilt until his command.
   d) no Jew was to work more than eight hours a day.

15) True or false: The rebuilding was stopped until the second year of the reign of King Darius.

16) When the Jews began rebuilding the temple during Darius's reign, did anyone question their actions?

17) The king said the Israelites were also to be given:
a) 30 minutes off to watch Hercules on TV each day.
b) whatever they needed to make sacrifices to God.
c) two daily servings each of ambrosia, food of the gods.
d) help from Hercules in building the temple.

PSALM 23

1) Did you know that although Psalm 23 was written before Christ was born, it speaks of Him?

2) True or false: The Book of Psalms should really be called the Book of Psalm.

3) Did you know Psalms is entitled "Praises" in the Hebrew text?

4) Is the Book of Psalms located in the Old Testament or the New Testament?

5) Did you know that if you open a standard King James Version Bible to the center, you will probably land somewhere in Psalms?

6) Who wrote Psalm 23?

7) True or false: David wrote all of the psalms.

8) What did David call the Lord in the first verse of Psalm 23?

9) In the Bible, Christians are sometimes referred to as:
   a) goats.
   b) vipers.
   c) serpents.
   d) sheep.

10) David may have sung the psalms as he played the:
   a) electric guitar.
   b) tuba.
   c) accordion.
   d) harp.

11) The Lord leads those He loves to:
   a) fame in Hollywood.
   b) money so they can buy anything they want.
   c) contentment.
   d) poverty.

12) David writes, "Yea, though I walk through the valley of the shadow of death, I will fear no evil: for thou art with me" (Psalm 23:4, KJV). After reading this, do you think David was a young shepherd boy when he wrote this psalm, or an old man reflecting upon his life?

13) Psalm 23 contains the popular expression "my cup runneth over" (verse 5). This means the author is:
   a) planning to sue a restaurant for serving too-hot coffee.
   b) joyful.
   c) forced to pay high dry-cleaning bills.
   d) clumsy.

14) Did you know Jesus promises Christians a life brimming with joy? In John 10:10 (KJV), He says, "I am come that they might have life, and that they might have it more abundantly."

15) In the psalm, "goodness and mercy" will follow David:
   a) until he catches the flu.
   b) until he gets a bad grade in school.
   c) all the days of his life.
   d) except on Tuesdays.

16) David says he will live forever in:
   a) the king's palace.
   b) the house of the Lord.
   c) Israel.
   d) a beach house.

17) True or false: The "house of the Lord" is another way of saying heaven.

GOD PROMISES A NEW KING

1) Who wrote the Old Testament Book of Zechariah?

2) You can find the Book of Zechariah in the:
   a) New Testament.
   b) Old Testament, after Genesis.
   c) Old Testament, after Haggai.
   d) Old Testament, before Zephaniah,
   since the books are listed
   alphabetically.

3) Zechariah was a:
   a) priest.   c) man of God.
   b) prophet.   d) all of the above.

4) Zechariah prophesied during the second year of Darius's reign (Zechariah 1:1). Zechariah and Haggai are the only Old Testament prophets to tell us they speak during the reign of a Gentile king. Most Old Testament prophets date their words during the rules of Israelite leaders.

5) In the beginning of his book, Zechariah says:
   a) the Lord has been very angry with your fathers.
   b) your fathers were just and fair.
   c) your fathers will be rewarded with great riches and glory.
   d) your fathers will appear in the movie *Twelve Tribes Are Enough*.

6) True or false: Zechariah was popular because he praised the Israelites.

7) Did Zechariah receive the word from the Lord that the people were to repent as the new temple was being built?

8) Another Old Testament prophet, Haggai, began his ministry in the second year of Darius's reign. (Haggai 1:1)

9) God says He will:
   a) destroy Jerusalem.
   b) allow Jerusalem to suffer a terrible military defeat.
   c) rain manna on the people.
   d) be merciful toward Jerusalem and allow the temple to be rebuilt.

10) The Lord spoke to Zechariah through:
   a) visions.
   b) a book.
   c) the Lord's Web page.
   d) dreams.

11) Whom does God tell Zechariah to crown king?

12) This king's name means:
   a) Dude.   c) Branch.
   b) Heirless.   d) Peacemaker.

13) This king will:
   a) own several dude ranches and let everyone ride his horses.
   b) marry six times and establish a new Christian church.
   c) branch out from his place and rebuild the temple.
   d) declare war to be illegal.

14) God promises Israel a bright future once they repent from their sin. Have you ever done wrong and then asked God for forgiveness? What happened? How did you feel?

NAVIGATING THE
NEW TESTAMENT

1) "And Jesus said unto them, 'Come ye after me, and I will make you to become fishers of men'" (Mark 1:17, KJV). Here Jesus was speaking to His disciples. Why is this an important verse for us today?

2) The ancient Greek text of the Old Testament is called the Septuagint Version. Most scholars believe it was recorded about 200 years before Christ was born.

3) The number of years between the end of the Old Testament and the beginning of the New Testament is:
   a) zero.
   b) 400.

   c) 1,000.
   d) not known.

4) True or false: When the New Testament was written, Israel was the largest and most powerful nation on earth.

5) Name the first four books of the New Testament, which are also known as the four Gospels.

6) The four Gospels tell about:
   a) the life and ministry of Jesus.
   b) Noah's ark.
   c) Paul's mission work.
   d) the gospel music industry.

7) True or false: Christians only need to read the four Gospels.

8) True or false: Jesus wrote all four Gospels.

9) In the four Gospels, we can find:
   a) stories Jesus told.
   b) Jesus' family lineage.
   c) accounts of Jesus' Resurrection.
   d) all of the above.

10) Who was the first person killed because he believed in Christ?

11) Some years are preceded by the abbreviation A.D., which means:
   a) after death.
   b) Antoinette and Dominic.
   c) after Domino's Pizza.
   d) *anno Domini*.

12) Did you know the New Testament was not put together as a collection of books until about A.D. 100?

13) What is a Gentile?
   (Are you a Gentile?)

14) The first missionary to the Gentiles was:
  a) Jim Elliot.   c) Paul the Apostle.
  b) Billy Graham.   d) John the Baptist.

15) Do you know a missionary who has traveled to share the Word of Christ? Perhaps you can visit the missionary or exchange letters so you can learn more about the mission field.

16) We can read about the travels of the first missionary to the Gentiles in the book:
a) *How to Tour Asia Minor on $1 a Day.*
b) Acts.
c) *Converting the Pagans: I Did It My Way.*
d) *Finding the Hidden Elegance of Prison Food.*

17) Paul the Apostle wrote many letters that are included in the New Testament. They give Christians instructions on how to:
a) get revenge on the Romans.
b) send attachments by e-mail.
c) love one another, behave, and conduct church business.
d) slip a file inside a bagel so he could break out of prison.

18) Why are these letters important to Christians today?

19) Throughout Paul's letters, he says Christians must have:
   a) love.
   b) husbands or wives.
   c) riches.
   d) funds to support his ministry.

20) True or false: We know for a fact that Paul wrote the Book of Hebrews.

21) The Book of Hebrews says:
   a) the Christian faith is better than all others.
   b) the Jewish faith is better than the Christian faith.
   c) Christians need to sacrifice two doves each Sunday.
   d) no Christian should watch television on Sunday.

22) True or false: The Books of James, 1 and 2 Peter, 1, 2, and 3 John, and Jude are all named after the people who wrote them.

23) The Epistle of James tells Christians how to:
   a) set up the Communion table.
   b) write a proper thank-you note.
   c) write a Sunday school curriculum for toddlers.
   d) live according to God's Word.

24) How many New Testament epistles are attributed to Peter?

25) True or false: Peter is considered to be the leader of Jesus' twelve disciples.

26) 1 Peter was written to help:
   a) raise money for new carpet in the sanctuary.
   b) Christians find other Christian businesses.
   c) suffering Christians.
   d) missionaries in South America.

27) True or false: According to Peter, you can trust any person who claims to be a Christian.

28) Peter wrote his second letter to help Christians:
   a) decide who are false teachers.
   b) determine who will be the best Bible translators.
   c) decide if they want to be missionaries.
   d) buy their first home.

29) True or false: Both John and Jude condemn
false teachers in their letters.

30) What is the last book of the New Testament?

DOVES

1) Did you know the first place a dove is mentioned in the Bible is Genesis 8:8? This is the story of the Great Flood.

2) Who built the ark to keep his family and the animals safe while God destroyed the earth with water?

3) True or false: The first bird Noah sent away from the ark was a dove.

4) Noah sent a dove out of the ark:
   a) to see if the waters had gone down so they could leave the ark.
   b) to find Dove Bars because they were hungry.
   c) to dig up some worms for the other birds on the ark.
   d) to symbolize peace in the world.

5) If Noah took in animals two by two, how could he send out a dove alone to search for receding water without wiping out the entire population of doves?

6) When the dove returned the first time, Noah knew:
   a) there was still too much water for them to leave the ark.
   b) the Dove Ice Cream factory had been declared a Federal Disaster Area.
   c) there were no worms.
   d) peace would not be possible just yet.

7) After the second trip, the dove brought Noah:
   a) an olive branch.
   b) a bar of vanilla ice cream covered with milk chocolate.
   c) a necklace.
   d) a slingshot.

8) True or false: Noah waited seven days between each time he sent the dove out from the ark.

9) Did the dove return after the third trip?

10) Doves were important in meeting many sacrificial requirements under Old Testament law. Throughout the books of the law in the Old Testament, you can find references that show God asked that doves be sacrificed to Him.

11) True or false: If you want to find out about Mosaic Law, you should read the Pentateuch.

12) In the Song of Solomon, the loved one is called a dove (2:14; 5:2; 6:9). What qualities do you think the loved one possesses?

13) After Jesus was baptized, the Holy Spirit descended upon Him like:
a) an angel.
b) a raven.
c) rain.
d) a dove.

14) Jesus said, "Behold, I send you forth as sheep in the midst of wolves: be ye therefore wise as serpents, and harmless as doves" (Matthew 10:16, KJV). This means:
a) God will protect you from every enemy.
b) don't let anything get in your way.
c) don't dress as a sheep for a costume party.
d) be wise, but do not hurt anyone.

15) In New Testament times, Jews still made animal sacrifices to God to atone for their sins under Mosaic Law. Why don't Christians make animal sacrifices today?

16) True or false: Jesus approved of the process of buying and selling sacrificial doves and other animals in the temple, since it was so convenient for everyone concerned.

17) Moneychangers were in the temple to:
   a) provide correct change.
   b) exchange one form of money for another.
   c) drum up support for Euromoney.
   d) take bets on races in the Coliseum.

18) Did you know Jesus referred to Isaiah 56:7 when he overturned the moneychangers' tables? "And he taught, saying unto them, 'Is it not written, My house shall be called of all nations the house of prayer?'" (Mark 11:17, KJV). Isaiah 56:7 (KJV) says, "Even them will I bring to my holy mountain, and make them joyful in my house of prayer: their burnt offerings and their sacrifices shall be accepted upon mine altar; for mine house shall be called an house of prayer for all people."

19) Jesus said the merchants had made the temple a:
   a) Cub Scout den.
   b) meeting place for den mothers.
   c) den of bears.
   d) den of thieves.

20) Think about how the dove is a symbol of the Holy Spirit. Do you see the Holy Spirit working in your life today? Do you see Him in the lives of those around you? If you're not sure, think about the fruits of the Spirit listed in Galatians 5:22–23 (NIV): "But the fruit of the Spirit is love, joy, peace, patience, kindness, goodness, faithfulness, gentleness and self-control." Someone with these qualities bears the fruit of the Holy Spirit.

TWO BLESSED PARENTS

1) Who were the earthly parents of Jesus Christ?

2) A listing of Jesus' ancestors, or His lineage, is found:
   a) in Matthew and Luke.
   b) in Mark and John.
   c) in Genesis and Revelation.
   d) in New York's Museum of Modern Art.

3) The two sources that trace Jesus' lineage differ from David to Jesus. This is because:
   a) neither one is accurate.
   b) the records in Bethlehem burned.
   c) one source had to guess at names after a computer crash.
   d) one traces Joseph's line from David, while the other traces Mary's ancestors.

4) Did you know Jesus is from the line of King David? Matthew lists Joseph as Mary's husband and Joseph was from the line of King David. Though Jesus is the son of Mary and the Holy Spirit, he is the legal son of Joseph. Therefore, Jesus is from the line of David.

5) Who told Mary she would bear a son?

6) True or false: The messenger did not know whether the baby would be a girl or a boy.

7) True or false: Mary and Joseph had been married for twenty years before she became pregnant by the Holy Spirit.

8) Joseph was a:
   a) circus performer.
   b) computer nerd.
   c) Pharisee.
   d) just, or honest, man.

9) When Joseph first discovered Mary's pregnancy, he:
   a) started to cry.
   b) set up a Web site so he could post baby pictures on the Internet.
   c) suggested Mary should be stoned.
   d) planned to break off the engagement quietly.

10) True or false: For Mary and Joseph, breaking off the engagement would not have been serious, since Mary had not purchased her wedding gown, hired caterers, or reserved The Country Club of Nazareth for the wedding reception.

11) Who convinced Joseph not to break off the engagement with Mary?

12) True or false: Joseph selected Jesus' name.

13) Why was the baby named Jesus?

14) Jesus is also called Emmanuel, meaning:
   a) firstborn.   c) God with us.
   b) Christmas.   d) man.

15) While she was expecting Jesus, Mary visited:
   a) a local herbalist.
   b) her cousin Elizabeth.
   c) Joseph's parents, to tell them she was sorry
      if they were embarrassed.
   d) a free health clinic.

16) True or false: Joseph immediately did what the
    Lord instructed.

17) Mary gave birth to Jesus in:
   a) the finest medical facility available, since
      Jesus is the Messiah.
   b) her home.
   c) the car, during a traffic jam.
   d) a stable because there was no room for
      them at the inn.

18) Did you know Simeon, a devout man who declared Jesus the Messiah soon after he was born, told Mary she would suffer along with her son. "Then Simeon blessed them and said to Mary, his mother: 'This child is destined to cause the falling and rising of many in Israel, and to be a sign that will be spoken against, so that the thoughts of many hearts will be revealed. And a sword will pierce your own soul too.'" (Luke 2:34–35, NIV).

19) True or false: Joseph and Mary reared Jesus as a Christian.

20) Did you know that when Jesus and Mary are mentioned together in the Bible, Jesus' name always appears first? (Matthew 2:11; 13–14; 20–21).

21) Jesus performed His first miracle at:
   a) Capernaum.
   b) Cana.
   c) Corinth.
   d) Caesarea.

22) The person who asked Jesus to perform this miracle was:
   a) Joseph.
   b) Mary.
   c) Elijah.
   d) a nervous bridegroom.

23) This miracle was important because it strengthened the faith of:
   a) Jesus' disciples.
   b) Jesus' earthly mother and father.
   c) His earthly sisters and brothers.
   d) the townspeople of Cana.

24) How many other sons did Mary have who are mentioned in the Bible? (We don't know the names of His earthly sisters.)

25) What was Joseph's profession?

26) Jesus grew up in:
   a) Bethlehem.
   b) Nazareth.
   c) Paris.
   d) Queens.

27) True or false: Because Joseph and Mary were powerful and influential, Jesus was always given a hero's welcome whenever He visited His hometown.

28) Since Joseph is not mentioned by name by the townspeople at the time they rejected Jesus, some scholars believe Joseph was not living at this time.

29) True or false: Another name for Jesus' mother is Mary Magdalene.

30) Did you know that even though God honored Mary and Joseph by allowing them to be Jesus' earthly parents, He did not honor them with fabulous riches, great power, or other earthly rewards? What do you think are the earthly rewards of Christians?
What is the Christian's reward in heaven?

JESUS TELLS US ABOUT ENEMIES

1) True or false: Jesus says we should not take revenge on our enemies, but ask God to get back at them instead.

2) Jesus says we should lend money to:
   a) our enemies, without expecting anything in return.
   b) our enemies, but only once.
   c) only our friends, since our enemies are mean.
   d) no one, since lending money is a bad practice.

3) True or false: Our reward for being kind to enemies will be a slap in the face.

4) Jesus says that God:
    a) shows mercy only to those who love
       Him.
    b) remembers only those who thank Him
       for His goodness.
    c) is kind to everyone, including the evil and
       unthankful.
    d) will destroy our enemies if we ask Him.

5) True or false: Jesus teaches that when people
   say mean things to you or about you, you
   should be kind to them anyway.

6) Did you know if there are people you don't
   like or get along with, you shouldn't feel
   alone? Jesus spends a lot of time teaching
   us how to treat enemies. That is because
   in a sinful world, it is impossible for
   everyone to get along with everyone
   else all the time.

7) Jesus says this of our Heavenly Father: "for he maketh his sun to rise on the evil and on the good, and sendeth rain on the just and on the unjust" (Matthew 5:45, KJV). What does this mean?

8) A publican is a:
   a) tax collector.
   b) celebrity.
   c) clerk at the public library.
   d) teacher at the public school.

9) Did you know Matthew, one of Jesus' twelve disciples, was a publican? "As he walked along, he saw Levi son of Alphaeus sitting at the tax collector's booth. 'Follow me,' Jesus told him, and Levi got up and followed him" (Mark 2:14, NIV). As you can see from the verse, Matthew was also known as Levi.

10) If we show love only to those who love us, we are no better than whom?

11) True or false: Since it was important that Jesus not damage His reputation as God's Son, he avoided associating with outcasts and sinners while here on earth.

12) Jesus teaches we should:
   a) not do anything extra for our enemies but the bare minimum.
   b) love our friends more than our enemies.
   c) give our enemies New Testament Bibles.
   d) go the extra mile for our enemies and to show them much love.

13) True or false: We don't have to forgive anybody who doesn't ask us for forgiveness.

14) When Jesus speaks of neighbors, He means:
   a) the people who live in the house next to yours.
   b) everyone.
   c) the people who live in your town.
   d) your enemies.

15) Jesus' teaching, "Thou shalt love thy neighbour as thyself," is what He called the second commandment (Matthew 22:39, KJV). This commandment applies to everyone, including our enemies, since enemies are also neighbors, regardless of where they live. This teaching means we are not to put our interests above those of others.

16) Jesus teaches the first great commandment is:
   a) don't get mad, get even.
   b) never forget the bad things someone has done to you.
   c) love God with all your heart, soul, and mind.
   d) don't let the sun go down on your anger.

17) What is the first of God's Ten Commandments?

18) Is Jesus' teaching about the first great commandment the same as the first commandment? How?

19) According to Jesus, people will know we are His disciples when we:
   a) get three perfect attendance pins at church.
   b) love one another.
   c) go to Vacation Bible School every year.
   d) listen to Christian radio stations every day.

20) Which of Jesus' disciples betrayed Him? (Hint: To betray means to deliver someone to an enemy.)

21) When Jesus' disciple betrayed Him, the disciple received:
   a) a free, all-expense-paid vacation.
   b) a houseful of new furniture.
   c) thirty pieces of silver.
   d) a chance to appear on a TV game show.

22) According to Matthew's Gospel, when Jesus was betrayed, He said:
a) "Friend, wherefore art thou come?"
b) "Verily, I am innocent!"
c) "Why dost thou kiss me on the cheek? Gross!"
d) "This means I'm down to eleven disciples."

ALL IN A DAY'S WORK

1) What is a parable?

2) Jesus taught in parables so:
   a) those who didn't love God wouldn't understand His teachings.
   b) He could put them together later in a book.
   c) His disciples could sell the rights to them after His Resurrection.
   d) He would be famous.

3) True or false: The disciples always understood the parables without Jesus having to explain them.

4) True or false: You can find Jesus' parables in the four Gospels.

5) Did you know the parable of the householder is recorded only in Matthew's Gospel?

6) A householder is:
   a) a maid.
   b) a collector of miniature houses.
   c) a real estate agent.
   d) the head of a house.

7) This parable describes:
   a) a day in the life of a stay-at-home mom.
   b) the Cinderella story.
   c) the kingdom of heaven.
   d) the fable of the tortoise and the hare.

8) What coin did the householder agree to pay each laborer for a day's work in his vineyard?

9) The coin the householder agreed to pay his workers was:
   a) the value of a day's pay.
   b) like a U.S. dime.
   c) the most common coin in use at that time.
   d) all of the above.

10) This parable speaks of a twelve-hour workday. The day probably started at 6 A.M. and ended at 6 P.M.

11) True or false: Throughout the day, the householder hired more laborers.

12) This parable speaks of day laborers, rather than people who had permanent jobs with the householder? Think about your life on earth in relation to living with God for eternity. We only serve God a short time here on earth, but the reward He gives us is great.

13) Late in the day, some laborers were still stand-
ing around because:
   a) they were lazy.
   b) they wanted to see who won the football
      game instead of working.
   c) no one had hired them.
   d) they were protesting the twelve-hour
      workday.

14) When the householder saw that the workers
were still there, he said:
   a) "Who would hire such lazy workers?"
   b) "Did the Washington Redskins or the Dallas
      Cowboys win the game?"
   c) "You also go and work in my vineyard."
   d) "I can't hear you!"

15) True or false: Every worker was paid for the
number of hours he worked.

16) True or false: The workers were paid in order
hired, from last to first.

17) When those who worked twelve hours saw that those who worked a short time received a whole day's wages, did they expect to be paid more than they were promised?

18) When the workers who had worked all day said they should receive more money, the householder told them:
a) to take their pay and go, since they were paid what they were promised.
b) he had deducted part of their pay to cover taxes and health insurance.
c) he would give each of them lunch money.
d) he was penalizing them for taking long coffee breaks.

19) True or false: The householder represents God.

20) Did you know some scholars think the workers who grumbled about their pay represent the Pharisees who opposed Jesus' teachings? They might also represent Christians who are faithful all their lives but wonder why God would give an equal reward to those who found Christ late in life.

21) The order the workers were paid is important because:
   a) the householder liked the latecomers best.
   b) the householder wanted to get rid of the slackers.
   c) it made the story harder for the Pharisees to interpret.
   d) those who are last on earth are first in heaven.

22) The householder's response to the grumblers is like God's in that:
  a) he is powerful and can do as he wishes.
  b) he is generous.
  c) he is willing to accept everyone.
  d) all of the above.

23) The grumblers were jealous and unhappy because the householder was generous. How does the householder's generosity in paying those who worked a short time compare to God's generosity to us?

24) The parable of the householder is similar to which other parable Jesus told?
a) The Good Samaritan. c) The Tares.
b) The Prodigal Son. d) The Dragnet.

25) Think about the parable of the householder. What does it say to you today?

MARTHA

1) Did you know there is no woman by the name of Martha in the Old Testament?

2) You can read about Martha in:
   a) the Gospel of John.
   b) John's first epistle.
   c) a book called *Martha's Vineyard*.
   d) the Gospels of Luke and John.

3) In what town did Martha live?

4) True or false: Martha was the sister of Lazarus, whom Jesus loved very much.

5) Martha was the sister of Mary, who:
   a) had perfumed Jesus' feet and wiped them with her hair.
   b) gave birth to Jesus.
   c) was also known as Mary Magdalene.
   d) brought her lamb to school.

6) When Jesus heard that Lazarus was sick, He:
   a) was convinced the sickness would end in death.
   b) knew the sickness would be to God's glory.
   c) diagnosed it as an upset stomach.
   d) developed a vaccine for the sickness.

7) True or false: As soon as Jesus heard Lazarus was sick, he rushed to Lazarus's house right away.

8) By the time Jesus arrived at Martha's house, Lazarus was:
   a) all better.
   b) dead.
   c) gone to California in search of gold.
   d) on a tour to promote his book, *Beyond Death: The Real Truth*.

9) When Martha heard Jesus was visiting, she:
   a) ran out to greet Him.
   b) changed the bed sheets so He would have a place to sleep.
   c) put on her best dress.
   d) prepared vegetable and tofu lasagna.

10) Meanwhile, Mary:
    a) went to the market to buy some perfume.
    b) washed her hair.
    c) called Bethany's Pizzeria to order Jesus'
       favorite pizza.
    d) stayed in the house.

11) True or false: Martha was convinced that if
    Jesus had been at the house, her brother
    would not have died.

12) True or false: When Jesus told Martha that
    Lazarus would
    rise again, she
    thought He
    meant Lazarus
    would rise again
    at the resurrec-
    tion at the last
    day.

13) "Jesus said unto her, 'I am the resurrection, and the life: he that believeth in me, though he were dead, yet shall he live: And whosoever liveth and believeth in me shall never die. Believest thou this?' " (John 11:25–26, KJV). What would you have answered?

14) After Martha told Mary that Jesus had arrived, Mary:
   a) spritzed on some of the perfume she had just bought.
   b) quickly dried her hair with a blow dryer.
   c) ran out to meet Jesus without delay.
   d) stayed in the house.

15) Why did those who came to comfort Mary think she had gone to cry at the grave of her brother (John 11:31)?

16) True or false: Like her sister Martha, Mary also told Jesus that Lazarus would not have died if He had been there.

17) Did you know the story of Lazarus contains the shortest verse in the entire Bible? That verse is John 11:35: "Jesus wept."

18) Why did Jesus weep?

19) The reaction in the crowd of mourners was mixed. Some marveled at how much Jesus loved Lazarus (John 11:36), while others remarked that Jesus, who had healed the blind, could have prevented Lazarus's death (John 11:37). Jesus' power was well known throughout the community.

20) The grave of Lazarus was:
  a) a vault in the family mausoleum (a building holding many bodies).
  b) six feet deep.
  c) in a shallow ditch.
  d) a cave, with a stone rolled over it.

21) When Jesus asked that the grave be opened, Martha said:
  a) "Lord, by this time he stinketh: for he hath been dead four days."
  b) "Let me fetch my brothers, who art stronger than I."
  c) "Lord, it is impossible, for I have no shovel."
  d) "I cannot, for I hath lost the key to the vault."

22) True or false: Martha agreed to open the grave after Jesus reminded her she should have faith.

23) Did Jesus raise Lazarus from the dead even though he had been dead for several days?

24) Was Martha present when her sister Mary anointed Jesus' feet with ointment and wiped them with her hair?

25) Judas Iscariot objected to Mary's costly act because the perfume could have been sold and the money:
   a) given to the poor.
   b) used to pay Martha for the dinner she had just catered for them.
   c) given to Jesus' parents, Mary and Joseph.
   d) used to buy gas for their tour bus.

26) The Bible says Judas objected in truth because:
   a) he was taking money from the disciples' funds for himself.
   b) was a member of Bethany's War on Waste recycling drive.
   c) wanted to purchase a stretch limo for them to ride in.
   d) wanted the perfume for himself.

27) Now that you have learned more about Judas Iscariot, are you surprised he was the disciple who betrayed Jesus?

28) Did you know that Bethany, the village where Martha lived, was only about two miles from Jerusalem?

29) True or false: Jesus visited Martha on at least one occasion.

30) When Mary did not help Martha prepare
dinner for Jesus, Martha:
a) did not complain.
b) wouldn't speak to Mary for several days.
c) asked Jesus to tell Mary
   to help her.
d) threw a vase at Mary.

31) What was Mary
doing rather than
helping Martha?

32) Jesus told Martha that:
   a) Mary was indeed very, very lazy.
   b) Mary wasn't very interesting anyway.
   c) He would buy her a new vase.
   d) she should allow Mary to listen to His Word.

33) Jesus' response to Martha meant:
   a) He liked Mary more than Martha.
   b) there is a time to worry about physical needs, and a time to listen to God.
   c) He felt sorry for Mary.
   d) she should hire a maid.

34) Have you ever felt stressed by activities, friends, and school? When you do, talk to the Lord about it.

A DISPUTE IN
THE EARLY CHURCH

1) We can read about the early Christian church in:
   a) the Book of Acts.
   b) the Book of Numbers.
   c) the Book of Exodus.
   d) the Book of Malachi.

2) A dispute arose in the early church which concerned:
   a) gleaning the fields for leftover harvest.
   b) Stephen's marriage.
   c) who would own the rights to broadcast films of Jesus' sermons.
   d) the widows' portion of bread.

3) Did you know most churches give food, shelter, or clothing to the poor as part of their community outreach? Think about ways your church and family help others.

4) True or false: The two groups of Jews involved in the dispute were the Hebrews and the Hellenists.

5) Hellenists were:
   a) early Christians who were eager to preach about the horridness of hell.
   b) members of a club all named Helen.
   c) members of the first motorcycle club.
   d) those who had adopted Greek culture.

6) Did you know this division emerged as a result of the conquests of Alexander the Great? His armies conquered Israel in 332 B.C. Alexander's goal was to make everybody adopt the language and culture of Greece.

7) How many men were chosen to distribute the bread?

8) Did you know all the men chosen to distribute the bread to the widows had Greek names? Why is this important?

9) How many of the men can you name? (Hint: One was the first person killed for being a Christian.)

10) Think about the dispute between the Hellenists and the Hebrews. What does their solution say about how to settle an argument?

THE ULTIMATE SACRIFICE

1) People who are persecuted are bothered, harassed, made fun of, annoyed, and sometimes even killed. Jesus said persecuted Christians are blessed because they will have:
   a) the kingdom of heaven.
   b) a supply of Rid-A-Pest.
   c) revenge.
   d) karate lessons.

2) In what famous sermon did Jesus make this statement?

3) Jesus' statement about persecution is part of what is known as the:
   a) Beatitudes.   c) Assertive Attitudes.
   b) Attitude Adjustments. d) Seattitudes.

4) True or false: Anyone who is persecuted for any reason will be blessed.

5) According to Jesus, what group of people was persecuted in the past? (Hint: Elijah belonged to this group of people.)

6) After Christ's Resurrection, the Romans were afraid of His new followers. The Romans worshiped many gods. Each god was responsible for a certain area of life, such as weather, war, and love. The Romans were afraid that if people didn't worship their gods, Rome would suffer hardship. That's why early Christians were persecuted.

7) In what book of the Bible can we read about Stephen?

8) This book of the Bible is located in the:
   a) Old Testament, after Genesis.
   b) New Testament, following the Gospel of John.
   c) end of the New Testament.
   d) end of the Old Testament.

9) True or false: Stephen was an evil man.

10) What is blasphemy?

11) Did you know blasphemy was a serious charge in Stephen's time? The penalty for blasphemy was death.

12) Stephen's enemies charged him with:
   a) blasphemy.
   b) singing off-key in the church choir.
   c) selling lottery tickets.
   d) charging too much for sacrificial doves.

13) True or false: The charges against Stephen were true.

14) During Stephen's trial, he looked like:
   a) a guilty prisoner.
   b) a bored young man.
   c) an angel.
   d) an angry young man.

15) Stephen answered the charge against him:
   a) by suing his accusers for ruining his reputation.
   b) by vowing to murder his enemies.
   c) by throwing himself on the mercy of the court.
   d) by giving a speech in defense of Christianity.

16) True or false: Stephen praised Israel during his court appearance.

17) After he spoke, Stephen saw:
   a) a large Bible in the sky.
   b) the Red Sea part.
   c) the glory of God and Jesus at God's right hand in heaven.
   d) Moses and Elijah.

18) How do we know this is what Stephen saw?

19) When the court heard Stephen's speech, they were:
a) angry.
b) fearful of the Lord.
c) moved to tears.
d) so emotional, they dropped the charges.

20) True or false: Stephen asked God to forgive the people who punished him.

21) Did you know Saul of Tarsus was present at Stephen's stoning? "And cast him out of the city, and stoned him: and the witnesses laid down their clothes at a young man's feet, whose name was Saul" (Acts 7:58).

22) Did Saul try to stop Stephen's stoning?

23) At the time of Stephen's death, Saul was:
   a) writing letters to the Christian churches.
   b) raising money for the Young Men's Mission Society at his church.
   c) putting Christians in prison.
   d) free on parole from prison.

24) True or false: Saul of Tarsus would later become the first missionary to the Gentiles.

25) Even though Stephen was unjustly accused of a crime and paid for it with his life, he asked God to forgive his enemies. Whose example was Stephen following?

THE EPHESIANS RECEIVE A LETTER

1) The Book of Ephesians is titled "The Epistle of Paul to the Ephesians." What is an epistle?

2) Paul was:
   a) one of Jesus' apostles.
   b) one of Jesus' original twelve disciples.
   c) the owner of an office supply store, so he had plenty of paper to write letters.
   d) a Christian from birth.

3) True or false: Paul always felt a special fondness for Christians and was kind to them all his life.

4) The Ephesians were:
   a) exotic pizza toppings.
   b) members of a baseball team, Ephesus Errors.
   c) members of the church at Ephesus.
   d) rich people who gave money to Paul's political party.

5) Did you know Ephesus was a city in the Roman province of Asia Minor? Today Asia Minor is part of modern Turkey. (Find Turkey on a map or globe.)

6) How do we know Paul wrote the letter to the Ephesians?

7) True or false: In this letter, Paul says he considers himself the greatest of Jesus' servants.

8) The mystery Paul writes of in Ephesians is that:
   a) he is Carolyn Keene, author of Nancy Drew mysteries.
   b) he never misses a rerun of detective show *Matlock*.
   c) Gentiles and Jews are equal.
   d) Jesus died only for the Gentiles.

9) True or false: In Ephesians, Paul reminds us that we all worship one God because all other gods are false.

10) When Paul refers to saints, he means:
    a) only those who have died.
    b) people who have helped him in the past.
    c) the New Orleans NFL football team.
    d) Christians.

11) Ephesians includes the famous quote "Speak the truth in love." What does this mean?

ANSWER KEY

THE OLD TESTAMENT

1) True.

2) True.

3) a) Pentateuch.

4) Moses wrote the first five books of the Bible.

6) (Exodus 20:1–17; Deuteronomy 5:7–21)
   c) Exodus and Deuteronomy.

7) The Ten Commandments are:
   (1) Thou shalt have no other gods before me.
   (2) Thou shalt not make unto thee any graven image.
   (3) Thou shalt not take the name of the LORD thy God in vain.
   (4) Remember the sabbath day, to keep it holy.
   (5) Honour thy father and thy mother.
   (6) Thou shalt not kill.
   (7) Thou shalt not commit adultery.
   (8) Thou shalt not steal.

(9) Thou shalt not bear false witness against thy neighbour.

(10) Thou shalt not covet.

8) (Genesis 1–2:7) a) creation of the universe.

9) In the Old Testament, the nation of Israel was divided into twelve tribes.

10) (Numbers 2:3–31) The twelve tribes were: Dan, Asher, Naphtali, Judah, Issachar, Zebulun, Reuben, Simeon, Gad, Ephraim, Manasseh, and Benjamin.

11) a) God gave the laws to Moses.

12) These records are important to show family lineage. Because of these records, we can trace Jesus' family line back to Adam and Eve.

13) d) illustrates two kinds of love. Ruth's loyalty to her mother-in-law, Naomi, is an example of love of family. As a result of staying with Naomi, Ruth found romance—the second kind of love—with a godly man named Boaz.

14) (Esther 2:2–9) b) won a beauty contest and married the king.

15) (Esther 9:26–32) True. Jewish people celebrate the Feast of Purim to remember how Esther saved her people at great risk to her own life.

16) (Job 42:12–17) b) God protects and rewards those who love Him.

17) True.

18) d) sings praises to God.

20) c) Proverbs.

21) False.

22) a) earth's glories fade, but God is forever.

23) False. We don't know who wrote Job, 1 and 2 Samuel, 1 and 2 Kings, or Esther.

24) Bible scholars study a long time to understand God's Book. They use their knowledge to piece together data like a puzzle. If the name of a king, judge, or other ruler is mentioned, we know the events took place during the time he ruled. Locations also help. For instance, since the first man and woman, Adam and Eve, were the only people ever to live in the Garden of Eden, we know their story takes place at the beginning of creation. The

language of the text is also important. For example, Hebrew text was generally written earlier than Greek text. Even with all this information, we still aren't sure who wrote some of the Bible books. If you enjoy history and puzzles, perhaps the Lord will someday call you to become a Bible scholar.

25) d) one sent by God to tell His plans for the future.

26) d) often is sent to warn God's people to repent of sin.

28) c) a big fish.

BREAD

1) False. In the New International Version of the Bible (NIV), bread is mentioned for the first time in Genesis 14:18: "Then Melchizedek king of Salem brought out bread and wine." The King James Version (KJV) mentions bread even earlier, in Genesis 3:19: "In the sweat of thy face shalt thou eat bread, till thou return unto the ground; for out of it wast thou taken: for dust thou art, and unto dust shalt thou return."

3) (Genesis 25:34) b) a bowl of lentil stew.

4) Esau sold his privileges as the firstborn son. In Bible
times, the eldest son usually inherited most of his
father's possessions. He also inherited his father's position of prestige in the community.

6) (Genesis 27) True.

7) (Genesis 27:1) a) old and blind.

8) (Genesis 27:11) They were fraternal twins. Jacob said. . .
"Esau is a hairy man, and I'm a man with smooth skin."

9) Exodus.

10) (Exodus 16:31) d) manna.

11) (Proverbs 31:27) b) idleness.

12) d) words of wisdom.

13) This verse means to trust the Lord with your life.

14) a) King Solomon.

15) a) Proverbs.

17) Jesus had been fasting for forty days, so He must have
been very, very hungry. He probably would have

enjoyed eating bread. But Satan's challenge was also tempting because the evil one wanted Jesus to prove He had the power to turn the stones into bread. Jesus resisted the temptation, overcoming both physical hunger and spiritual pride.

18) Although we need to feed our bodies food such as bread, we need to learn about God and obey His commandments. We can do this by going to church and Sunday school, reading the Bible, and talking to other Christians about God.

19) Deuteronomy 8:3.

20) When you are tempted to do wrong, always think about what God would want you to do. Pray about it. The goodness of God overcomes all evil.

21) "Our Father which art in heaven, Hallowed be thy name. Thy kingdom come. Thy will be done in earth, as it is in heaven. Give us this day our daily bread. And forgive us our debts, as we forgive our debtors. And lead us not into temptation, but deliver us from evil: For thine is the kingdom, and the power, and the glory, for ever. Amen" (Matthew 6:9–13, KJV). This prayer can also be found in Luke 11:2–4. Some versions read, "And forgive us our trespasses, as we forgive those who trespass against us."

22) This prayer asks for enough bread to eat today. It does not ask God to make us rich or to give us plenty to eat well into the future. Rather than being overly concerned about the future, we should take each day as a gift from God and live in accordance with His will. This does not mean we should be irresponsible. We should not do foolish things that would be bad for our future. For instance, it would be more fun to watch TV than to study. However, it is better to study when we know there's a test tomorrow.

23) (John 6:47–48) c) the bread of life.

24) The special sacrament is called Communion.

NOT EXACTLY JUDGE JUDY

1) In the Book of Judges.

3) False. Deborah was an exception.

4) (Judges 4:4) d) prophet.

5) (Judges 4:1) False.

6) (Judges 4:3) a) made life very hard for the Israelites.

7) (Judges 4:3) King Jabin had 900 iron chariots.

8) (Judges 4:3) They were slaves to King Jabin for twenty years.

9) (Judges 4:1, NIV) They were doing "evil in the eyes of the LORD." Though God punishes those who do evil, He also forgives those who ask for forgiveness and repent of their sins.

10) (Judges 4:6) True.

11) (Judges 4:6–7) c) deliver the enemy into the hands of Israel's general.

12) Mount Tabor was located in Galilee, on the borders of Naphtali and Zebulun. Some of the men in the army who were to defeat Sisera were from Naphtali and Zebulun.

14) (Judges 4:6–7) c) a general in Israel's army.

15) (Judges 4:8) a) Deborah, to ensure success. Deborah had already proposed taking 10,000 men, but Barak was afraid of defeat, even with such a large army.

16) (Judges 4:9) b) a woman.

17) False. Men were the heads of Jewish households. Women could not speak for themselves in legal matters. Women were spoken for by their fathers, husbands, sons, or closest male relative.

18) (Judges 4:16) Yes.

19) a) the fifth chapter of Judges.

TALKING TO GOD

1) True. God listens to us any time of the day or night. Sometimes we might say a quick prayer when we need help. Other times, we might utter a short prayer of thanks for a beautiful day or a special blessing. Still on other occasions God may lead us to say a prayer even though we weren't thinking of praying to Him even moments before. No matter how many quick prayers we say during the day, though, it is always good to take time with the Lord each day for a time of unhurried prayer.

2) a) praise Him. God likes for us to glorify and praise Him. This is shown by the many sacrifices He required in the Old Testament.

3) The Book of Psalms.

4) a) David.

6) False. (Check out Genesis 24:12, 25:21; 1 Samuel 8:6; there are many more!)

7) (Genesis 24:12) True.

8) (Genesis 25:21) d) Rebekah to have a baby.

10) The word sovereign shows Moses knows God is ruler over all. "Overlook the stubbornness of this people, their wickedness and their sin" shows he knows the people of Israel had been sinful.

11) a) be humble. Each and every one of us is lowly in comparison to God. By admitting this to God, we are showing Him we know He is great.

15) False. Most of them proved to be wicked. You can read about the kings of Israel in 1 and 2 Kings and in 1 Chronicles.

16) (Jonah 1:17) a) was swallowed by a big fish.

17) (Jonah 2:1) True.

19) True. (See Mark 1:35 as one example) Jesus got up before the sun rose to spend time alone with God. This

may have been the only time he had to be alone with God the Father during an average day.

20) (Luke 5:16) b) alone.

21) Pharisees were members of a Jewish sect who knew Mosaic Law. They tried to adhere to it and enforce it "to the letter." Because Jesus overruled some of the points of Mosaic Law, he angered the Pharisees.

22) (Luke 18:11) a) loudly, boasting about his goodness.

23) (Luke 18:13) b) admitted his sin and asked God for mercy.

24) In Jesus' day, tax collectors often charged people more money in taxes than they owed. The tax collectors then pocketed the difference. People resented the tax collectors for becoming rich through such dishonesty.

25) (Luke 18:14) False.

26) (Matthew 5:38–39) False.

27) (Matthew 5:43–44) d) all of the above.

28) True. When you pray to God, always remember to thank Him for His goodness and mercy as well. There are many examples of thanks given in prayer in the

Bible. They are most evident in Psalms since that is a book of praise and prayer.

A WICKED KING

2) False. Very few of the kings pleased God.

4) (1 Kings 16:31) b) worshiped the god Baal.

5) a) fertility. The people thought if they worshiped Baal, they would have good harvests and plenty of food to eat.

6) (1 Kings 16:31) b) Jezebel.

7) (1 Kings 16:31) False. Jezebel was evil and did not influence Ahab to worship the true God, the God of Israel.

8) (1 Kings 16:30–33) True.

9) (1 Kings 17:1) c) God commanded it to rain.

11) (1 Kings 18:20–21) True.

12) According to *Webster's Dictionary,* a vineyard is "a planting of grapevines."

13) (I Kings 21:2) a) it was near his palace and he wanted to use it as a vegetable garden.

14) (I Kings 21:2) a) a better vineyard or to pay him what it was worth.

15) (I Kings 21:3) d) God refused to let Naboth give King Ahab the land.

16) (I Kings 21:4) c) sulked and refused to eat.

17) (I Kings 21:9) True.

18) (I Kings 21:14) Yes.

19) (I Kings 21:16) a) took it.

20) (I Kings 21:19) True. God is never, ever, fooled.

21) (I Kings 21:17) Elijah.

22) (I Kings 21:19) True.

23) The Bible does not say Jezebel wanted the vineyard for herself or cared anything about it. Ahab probably did not know about Jezebel's plan until Naboth was dead. However, once he found out Naboth died, Ahab did not tell Jezebel she was wrong. Since Ahab took the

vineyard for himself as soon as Naboth died, he bene-fited from his wife's plan. That is why Ahab was to blame for Naboth's death. This means if someone does something bad so we can get our way, it would be wrong to go along with it.

MEET ELIJAH

1) a) 1 Kings, chapter 17, verse 1.

2) c) a prophet.

4) (1 Kings 17:1) True.

5) (1 Kings 17:1) d) no rain for the next few years until God commanded rain to fall.

6) (1 Kings 16:30) God was angry with King Ahab because he was evil.

7) (1 Kings 16:30) False.

8) (1 Kings 16:31–32) b) worshiped the god Baal.

10) (1 Kings 17:3) c) east of Jordan.

11) a) Elijah's prophecy had made King Ahab mad.

12) (1 Kings 17:4) a) ravens.

13) God controls the earth and every creature living here. He has the power to command any being to do His bidding.

14) (1 Kings 17:6) d) bread and meat in the morning and evening. (The Bible does not tell us what kind of bread and meat the ravens brought.)

15) (1 Kings 17:9) b) a widow.

16) (1 Kings 17:7) The brook dried up because, as God had promised, there was no rain.

17) (1 Kings 17:12–14) False.

18) (1 Kings 17:21) d) prayed to God. (This is the same widow who had fed Elijah while he was in hiding.)

19) (1 Kings 17:23) True.

21) (Matthew 16:14) d) all of the above. This answer (see also Mark 8:28; Luke 9:19) given by Jesus' disciples shows there was confusion about Jesus. Since He healed people and performed miracles, some thought Jesus was one of the prophets risen from the dead. The confusion is especially evident when you remember that Jesus was born six months after John the Baptist (Luke 1:41) and was

baptized by him (Matthew 3:13; Mark 1:9). Since they lived on earth at the same time, there is no way Jesus could have been John the Baptist. The disciples knew who Jesus was, however. We are to remember Peter's answer: "And Simon Peter answered and said, 'Thou art the Christ, the Son of the living God'" (Matthew 16:16, KJV).

22) (Matthew 17:1–3) True. This miracle of God is called the Transfiguration.

23) The disciples answer this with a question they asked Jesus: "The disciples asked him, 'Why then do the teachers of the law say that Elijah must come first?'" (Matthew 17:10, NIV). The return of Elijah, a revered Old Testament prophet, was to signal the coming of the Jewish Messiah.

24) True. These are Jesus' own words: "But I say unto you, That Elias is come already, and they knew him not, but have done unto him whatsoever they listed" (Matthew 17:12, KJV). This means John the Baptist was the Elijah, but the people did not recognize him.

GOD PROVIDES FOR THE POOR

1) False. Many of God's Old Testament laws contained provisions for the poor.

2) b) charging people interest, or extra money, to borrow money. This means that if you lend someone money, you will ask that person to pay you back more in return. For example, if you loan a friend $1.00 and ask her to pay you back $1.25, you are asking for 25 cents in interest.

3) (Exodus 22:25) No. Today, credit is extended for many purchases and interest is paid to banks in return for use of their money. This is different from the Old Testament instruction not to charge poor people interest. This law was meant to keep rich people from taking advantage of poor people who could not pay them back easily. Note that the credit card had not been invented in Old Testament times, as well as large appliances, cars, and other big-ticket items. Therefore, borrowing large amounts of money was seldom necessary as it is today. The general practice in Old Testament times was not to borrow money except in extreme emergencies.

4) (Luke 6:34) d) if you make a loan, do not expect repayment.

5) (Exodus 23:2–3) False. Though God protected the poor in the provisions of the Mosaic Law, He did not extend the protection to favoritism or unfair treatment of the rich.

6) (Leviticus 19:9–10) b) gather leftover crops after the harvest.

7) (Ruth 2:23) Ruth.

9) (Deuteronomy 24:15) d) before sundown at the end of each workday. Since the poor had no extra money to spare, this was the Lord's way of giving them their daily provision.

10) True. The story appears in 2 Samuel, chapter 11. David was guilty of using his power and position as a king to take his soldier's wife.

11) (2 Samuel 12:1–7) a) a rich man and a poor man.

13) "Jesus said unto him, 'If thou wilt be perfect, go and sell that thou hast, and give to the poor, and thou shalt have treasure in heaven: and come and follow me' " (Matthew 19:21, KJV).

14) (Matthew 19:22) d) walked away with sadness, for he owned much.

15) (Matthew 26:10) a) said she had done something good for Him.

17) (Matthew 26:8–9) True.

19) (Mark 12:43–44) The widow's offering was a true sacrifice. By giving all her money to the treasury, she was trusting in God to provide for her needs. The rich people who gave a lot of money had plenty left at home to provide for their needs and luxuries. So in proportion to their incomes, they did not give as much as the widow.

20) (Luke 6:20) True.

21) (Luke 16:20–21) a) did not show him any mercy. Though the Bible does not say so directly, it is implied the man did not feed Lazarus.

22) (Luke 16:23) True.

23) (1 Corinthians 13:3) d) no matter how much you give to the poor, it's no good without love. (Note: In the King James Version, "charity" is the same as love.)

GOD'S SPECIAL DAYS

1) (Exodus 12:17) True.

2) a) without yeast.

3) (Exodus 12:17) c) how God brought the Israelites out of Egypt.

4) (Exodus 12:17) Exodus.

6) (Exodus 12:18–19) Seven days.

7) (Exodus 12:20) False.

9) True. The terms Passover and Feast of Unleavened Bread were sometimes used interchangeably.

10) (Exodus 12:13) a) lamb's blood.

11) False. Since the Exodus is the cornerstone of the Jewish faith, most Jews still observe Passover. In fact, most calendars sold in America mark Passover. Can you find the date of this year's Passover on your calendar? It should occur in March or April. The date changes each year because Passover follows the lunar cycle.

13) (Numbers 28:16–17) a) the day after Passover.

14) (Matthew 26:2; Mark 14:1) True.

15) (Matthew 26:2–5) c) were afraid the Jews might riot. (By this time, Jesus was proclaiming that He is God's Son and was called the King of the Jews. Because it was

customary for Jews to travel to the city to celebrate the Passover, Jerusalem had more Jewish people than usual. Jesus' enemies believed they would not be able to control such a large, angry mob should Jesus be arrested during the feast.)

16) (John 18:38) False.

17) (John 18:39) d) release one prisoner.

18) (John 18:40) False. Barabbas was a common criminal who had been involved in a rebellion. Jesus knew it was time for Him to be crucified, so He did not resist God's will.

20) (1 Corinthians 5:7) False. We do not need a Passover lamb since Christ has already died for our sins.

22) (Exodus 23:16) True. In this way, the Lord's bounty would be remembered all year.

24) (Leviticus 23:23–24) True.

25) (Leviticus 23:27) d) make amends for their sins. (On this day, the sins of the past year were to be reconciled and forgiven.)

26) True. It is a reverent, serious day of fasting and prayer. Look on your calendar for the day marked Yom Kippur.

27) (Leviticus 23:39–43) c) the forty years' wandering in the wilderness.

28) (Leviticus 23:42–43) c) booths.

29) Christians don't celebrate these holidays because we rejoice in our Lord and Savior, Jesus Christ. He is the sacrificial lamb who atoned for our sins; we cannot atone for our own sins. Only Jesus can do that.

A NEW TEMPLE

2) False. Ezra's name is never mentioned.

3) a) the Old Testament, just before Nehemiah.

4) b) the end of the Jews' captivity in Babylon.

5) (Ezra 1:2) King Cyrus of Persia decreed the temple would be built.

6) (Ezra 2: 64–65) 49,897.

7) False. Israel's enemies—probably the Samaritans and Cutheans—opposed it.

8) **False.** Because the nation of Israel was not as wealthy as it was during David and Solomon's time, there were not as many materials to build a grand structure.

9) **b) Persia.**

10) **No.** Though Israel's enemies had opposed the rebuilding of the temple for many years, it was Artaxerxes who put a halt to its construction.

11) **(Ezra 4:8)** c) sending a letter.

12) **(Ezra 4:19)** d) rebellious.

13) **Yes.** They rebelled once against the Assyrians (2 Kings 18:7) and twice against Babylon (2 Kings 24:1, 20).

14) **(Ezra 4:21)** c) the city not be rebuilt until his command.

15) **(Ezra 4:24)** True.

16) **(Ezra 4:3–7)** Yes. They were questioned by the governor of the region, who then sent a letter to King Darius.

17) **(Ezra 6:9,10)** b) whatever they needed to make sacrifices to God. (Note that the king is not entirely unselfish. He wants the Israelites to pray for the health of himself and his heirs. Even though the Persians did not worship

Jehovah, this request is not surprising. In Old Testament times, people routinely worshiped all gods in hopes of being blessed and protected by all of them.)

PSALM 23

2) False. The Book of Psalms should be referred to in the plural, meaning more than one, since it contains many individual psalms (such as Psalm 23).

4) In the Old Testament, after Job.

6) King David.

7) False. Although he wrote over seventy of the psalms, others contributed to this book. Some of the authors are anonymous.

8) (Psalm 23:1) A shepherd.

9) (Matthew 25:31–34) d) sheep.

10) (1 Samuel 16:23) d) harp.

11) (Psalm 23:2) c) contentment. (As a shepherd leads his sheep to a safe resting place, food [lie down in green

pastures], and drink [still waters], so Jesus meets the needs of Christians.)

12) Although Bible scholars have not been able to pinpoint the exact date of authorship, we can assume that the psalm was written late in David's life since he seems to think his death will happen soon. The psalm is filled with the kind of wisdom gained from living a full and long life.

13) b) joyful. His happiness and prosperity is so great, he has more than he could possibly need.

15) (Psalm 23:6) c) all the days of his life. (Like David, we all make mistakes. But if we believe in Jesus, God has promised never to leave us. He will truly love us all the days of our lives.)

16) (Psalm 23:6) b) the house of the LORD.

17) (John 14:2) True.

GOD PROMISES A NEW KING

1) Zechariah.

2) c) Old Testament, after Haggai.

3) d) all of the above.

5) (Zechariah 1:2) a) the Lord has been very angry with your fathers.

6) (Zechariah 1:1–6) False. He called them to repent from the wicked ways of previous generations.

7) (Ezra 6:1–15) Yes. We know this because he speaks late in the second year King Darius ruled, and King Darius allowed the temple building to resume.

9) (Zechariah 1:16) d) be merciful toward Jerusalem and allow the temple to be rebuilt.

10) a) visions. (Note: Dreams occur while the person is asleep, and visions occur when the person is awake. The Lord used symbols to show Zechariah, when he was fully awake, His plan for His people. Zechariah asks the angel who visits him what the symbols mean. The Book of Zechariah is easier to understand than some other books relying on symbols, such as Revelation. Read the first six chapters of Zechariah to find out all the details of the visions. Talk to another Christian about this book and its symbols.)

11) (Zechariah 6:11) Joshua. (Note: This is not the same Joshua of the Book of Joshua.)

12) (Zechariah 6:12) c) branch.

13) (Zechariah 6:12) c) branch out from his place and rebuild the temple.

NAVIGATING THE NEW TESTAMENT

1) If we spread the Gospel and tell others about Christ, we, too, will become fishers of men.

3) b) 400. This is called the intertestamental period, or the silent years. During this time, society changed so that the New Testament world was much different from the Old Testament world. This explains why the New Testament was written in different languages and reflects different customs.

4) False. Israel was no longer an independent nation but a province of a larger empire.

5) The four Gospels are Matthew, Mark, Luke, and John.

6) a) the life and ministry of Jesus.

7) (2 Timothy 3:16) False. God speaks to us through all the books of the Bible. We must know His entire Word to be faithful.

8) False. Jesus did not write any of the Gospels.

9) d) all of the above.

10) (Acts 7:59) Stephen.

11) d) *anno Domini. Anno Domini* means "in the year of the Lord." This means the year falls in the Christian era, after the birth of Christ.

13) A Gentile is a non-Jew. In Jesus' time, since most Gentiles worshiped false gods, the Jewish people looked down upon them as pagans.

14) (Acts 9:10–15) c) Saul, later known as Paul the Apostle.

16) b) Acts (or The Acts of the Apostles).

17) c) love one another, behave, and conduct church business.

18) Even though they were written almost 2,000 years ago, the instructions contained in Paul's letters are still timely. For example, we should always love one another. How we present ourselves as individuals and as members of a church is a witness for Christ. The world watches us. We must live as Christ wants us to live—and Paul tells us how.

19) (1 Corinthians 13:1–13) a) love.

20) False. Bible scholars are not sure who wrote the Book of Hebrews.

21) a) the Christian faith is better than all others.

22) True.

23) d) live according to God's Word.

24) Two New Testament epistles: 1 and 2 Peter.

25) (Matthew 16:18) True.

26) c) suffering Christians.

27) (2 Peter 2:1) False.

28) a) decide who are false teachers.

29) True.

30) Revelation.

DOVES

2) (Genesis 7:5) Noah built the ark, according to God's instructions.

3) (Genesis 8:7) False. The first bird Noah sent was a raven.

4) (Genesis 8:8) a) to see if the waters had gone down so they could leave the ark.

5) (Genesis 7:2–3) God provided several pairs of some species. Also, since the ark was adrift for almost a year, it is possible that babies were born on the ark.

6) (Genesis 8:9) a) there was still too much water for them to leave the ark.

7) (Genesis 8:11) a) an olive branch.

8) (Genesis 8:10, 12) True.

9) (Genesis 8:12) No.

11) True. These are the first five books of the Old Testament. Most of Mosaic Law is recorded in Exodus and Leviticus.

12) The loved one most likely is calm, gentle, tender, and peaceful.

13) (Matthew 3:16) d) a dove.

14) d) be wise, but do not hurt anyone.

15) Through His crucifixion, Jesus served as the perfect lamb, the ultimate sacrifice, and washed away our sins. As a result, Christians do not need to make animal sacrifices to God.

16) (Mark 11:15) False.

17) b) exchange one form of money for another. According to Bible scholars, this allowed foreigners to exchange their form of money for the kind needed to pay the temple tax.

19) (Mark 11:17) d) den of thieves.

TWO BLESSED PARENTS

1) Mary and Joseph.

2) (Matthew 1:1–16; Luke 3:23–38) a) in Matthew and Luke.

3) d) one traces Joseph's line from David, while the other traces Mary's ancestors. (Matthew traces Joseph's line,

while Luke traces Mary's. In a time when lineage was traced only through men, going back through Mary's line was unusual. Some scholars think this is because Luke wanted to emphasize Mary's importance. Joseph's line shows Jesus' legal lineage since Jesus was legally recognized as Joseph's son. His blood lineage is traced through Mary. If you answered that neither source is accurate, remember that the Bible is the true, inspired, inerrant word of God.)

5) (Luke 1:28) an angel.

6) (Luke 1:32) False.

7) False. Mary and Joseph were engaged to be married.

8) (Matthew 1:19) d) just, or honest, man.

9) (Matthew 1:19) d) planned to break off the engagement quietly. (Note: It is important to understand that Mary had not violated any marriage or engagement vows. God chose a righteous woman to bear His son, not someone who would disregard His commandments.)

10) False. An engagement was more difficult to break than it is today. As Matthew 1:19 indicates, Mary would have been disgraced if the engagement were broken.

11) (Matthew 1:20) Either "an angel" or "God" would be correct, since angels are God's messengers.

12) (Matthew 1:21) False. The angel told Joseph what Jesus' name would be.

13) (Matthew 1:21) The name Jesus means "Savior," or one who shall save His people from their sins.

14) (Matthew 1:23) c) God with us.

15) (Luke 1:39–40) b) her cousin Elizabeth.

16) (Matthew 1:24) True.

17) (Luke 2:7) d) a stable because there was no room for them at the inn.

19) False. Jesus was reared in the Jewish faith. Christianity was not established until after Jesus' Resurrection.

21) (John 2:1) b) Cana.

22) (John 2:3) b) Mary.

23) (John 2:11) a) Jesus' disciples.

24) (Matthew 13:55) four.

25) (Matthew 13:55; Mark 6:3) He was a carpenter.

26) b) Nazareth.

27) (Matthew 13:55–58) False.

29) (Luke 8:2) False. Mary Magdalene was one of Jesus' followers.

30) (John 14:2) Living with God in heaven is our reward.

JESUS TELLS US ABOUT ENEMIES

1) (Luke 6:35) False.

2) (Luke 6:35) a) our enemies, without expecting anything in return.

3) (Luke 6:35) False. Sometimes when you are nice to your enemies, you may feel as though your reward is even more insult and injury. Since this is a fallen world, people are not always nice to you just because you are nice to them. However, sometimes God allows you to receive an earthly reward when a person you are nice to changes his or her mind and becomes your friend. Whether or not this happens, though, those who follow Jesus' teachings will be rewarded in heaven as He promises.

4) (Luke 6:35) c) is kind to everyone, including the evil and unthankful.

5) (Matthew 5:45) True. Since this teaching goes against the ways of the sinful world, it is probably best to bless your enemies in private. Pray alone to God about them. Talk about it with another Christian you trust.

7) This means that God does not favor one person over another.

8) a) tax collector.

10) (Matthew 5:46–47) Jesus says we are no better than the publicans, some of the most hated people of His time. Publicans were known for charging too much tax and keeping the extra money for themselves. In addition, publicans worked for the Roman government, which was ruled by people who did not love the Lord. Just like it was easy for the publicans to rob the people, so it's easy for us to love only those who love us. Jesus wants us to take the extra step and be kind to people who don't care about us, as well as those who do.

11) (Mark 2:15) False. Jesus put His teachings into practice. People did not expect the Son of God to eat freely with sinners but to seek out the righteous.

12) (Luke 6:29) d) go the extra mile for our enemies and to show them much love.

13) (Luke 6:37) False. God is everyone's ultimate judge, and He knows each person's heart. The issue of forgiveness is for Him to decide. God will remember how we respond to other people when it is time for Him to reward us in heaven.

14) b) everyone. (Jesus means all people, regardless of where they live, and regardless of whether you like them or not.)

16) (Matthew 22:37) c) love God with all your heart, soul, and mind.

17) (Exodus 20:3, KJV) "Thou shalt have no other gods before me."

18) Yes. These teachings are the same, even though the words are different. God says He is the Lord and we should not love any other god more than we love Him. Today that includes modern idols such as celebrities and things money can buy. Anything, including television, sports, and video games, can become an idol when it takes up too much of our time, thoughts, and energy—and takes us away from God.

19) (John 13:34–35) b) love one another.

20) Judas Iscariot.

21) (Matthew 26:15) c) thirty pieces of silver. (Note: Thirty pieces of silver were worth about 120 denarii, or four months' wages in the first century.)

22) (Matthew 26:50) a) "Friend, wherefore art thou come?" Even in His time of betrayal, Jesus still addressed Judas as "Friend." This shows how Jesus followed his own difficult teachings regarding enemies.

ALL IN A DAY'S WORK

1) A parable is a story that imparts a lesson.

2) (Matthew 13:11–13) a) those who didn't love God wouldn't understand His teachings.

3) (Matthew 13:36) False.

4) False. None of the parables appears in the Gospel of John.

6) d) the head of a house. (Note: The NIV version of the Bible substitutes the word landowner for householder.)

7) (Matthew 20:1) c) the kingdom of heaven.

8) (Matthew 20:2) Either a penny (KJV) or a denarius (NIV) is correct. Both translations refer to the same coin, which was a day's wages for a laborer at the time.

9) d) all of the above.

11) (Matthew 20:3–6) True. He hired more in the third, sixth, ninth, and eleventh hours.

13) (Matthew 20:7) c) no one had hired them.

14) (Matthew 20:4, 7) c) "You also go and work in my vineyard."

15) (Matthew 20:9) False.

16) (Matthew 20:8) True.

17) (Matthew 20:11–12) Yes.

18) (Matthew 20:14) a) to take their pay and go, since they were paid what they were promised.

19) True.

21) (Matthew 20:16) d) those who are last on earth are first in heaven.

22) d) all of the above. God is all powerful and in control of everything. He may do as He wishes, for He created heaven and earth. As the householder continued to look for laborers throughout the day, God looks for new people to follow Him throughout time. His door is always open to those who love Him, repent of their sins, and accept Jesus Christ as their Savior.

23) Sometimes God's ways do not seem fair to us. We might be jealous that some Christians seem to have more privileges, possessions, or better grades than we do. However, God is generous to us, too. Think about all that God has done for you.

24) b) The Prodigal Son. The second son squandered his inheritance and came back much later to ask the father's forgiveness. The older son, who had stayed faithful to the father all along, was angry that his younger brother was taken back with a big celebration, thereby rewarded even though he had been faithless. The older son is like the grumblers in the parable of the householder. Jesus taught the same lessons in several different stories to help people understand. Read about The Good Samaritan in Luke 10:30–37; The Prodigal Son in Luke 15:11–32; The Wheat and the Tares in Matthew 13:24–30; and The Dragnet in Matthew 13:47–50.

MARTHA

2) (Luke 10:38–41; John 11:1–44,12:2) d) the Gospels of Luke and John.

3) (John 11:1) Bethany.

4) (John 11:3) True.

5) (John 11:2) a) had perfumed Jesus' feet and wiped them with her hair.

6) (John 11:4) b) knew the sickness would be to God's glory.

7) (John 11:6) False. He did not leave where he was for two days.

8) (John 11:17) b) dead.

9) (John 11:20) a) ran out to greet Him.

10) (John 11:20) d) stayed in the house.

11) (John 11:21) True.

12) (John 11:24) True.

14) (John 11:29) c) ran out to meet Jesus without delay.

15) (John 11:30) They had not yet seen Jesus. In her eagerness to greet him, Martha had met Jesus outside of town. He had not yet arrived in town when Mary left the house.

16) (John 11:32) True.

18) He wept because he was sad that Lazarus had died.

20) (John 11:38) d) a cave, with a stone rolled over it.

21) (John 11:39) a) "Lord, by this time he stinketh: for he hath been dead four days."

22) (John 11:40) True.

23) (John 11:44) Yes.

24) (John 12:2–3) Yes.

25) (John 12:5) a) could have been given to the poor.

26) (John 12:6) a) he was taking money from the disciples' funds for himself.

27) Judas' betrayal of Jesus should come as no surprise since he was dishonest all along.

29) (Luke 10:38) True.

30) (Luke 10:40) c) asked Jesus to tell Mary to help her.

31) (Luke 10:39) She was listening to Jesus.

32) (Luke 10:41–42) d) she should allow Mary to listen to His Word.

33) b) there is a time to worry about physical needs, and a time to listen to God.

A DISPUTE IN THE EARLY CHURCH

1) a) the Book of Acts.

2) d) the widows' portion of bread. (Note: At this time, the church distributed food to those in the Christian community who were not able to provide for themselves. In this case, one group of Jews believed the widows in their group were not being given as much bread as those in another group. Stephen, one of the early Christians, was among the holy men chosen to distribute bread.)

4) (Acts 6:1) True.

5) d) those who had adopted Greek culture.

7) (Acts 6:5) seven.

8) This indicates that the Jews selected to distribute the bread were probably Hellenists. Obviously the Hebrews were willing to let the Hellenists be in charge of distributing bread not only to Hellenist widows but their own Hebrew widows as well. A true compromise would have divided the number of men between the Hebrews and the Hellenists. However, the church leaders took the extra step of generosity by choosing all Hellenists. As a result, the dispute was settled, and the early church continued to grow.

9) (Acts 6:5) The seven men were Stephen, Philip, Prochorus, Nicanor, Timon, Parmenas, and Nicolas.

10) Considering the other person's viewpoint is key to settling a dispute. When we are mad, controlling our emotions is very important. We should step back and consider the argument. How does the other person see the situation? What will happen if we "win" the argument? What will happen if we don't? If we think about it, most arguments are not worth winning, especially if it means losing a friend. Think about what would have happened if the dispute about the bread had not been solved. The Christian faith would have suffered a huge setback over an issue that was not even of eternal importance!

THE ULTIMATE SACRIFICE

1) (Matthew 5:10) a) the kingdom of heaven.

2) The Sermon on the Mount.

3) (Matthew 5:3–12) a) Beatitudes.

4) (Matthew 5:10) False. People can be persecuted for many reasons, but it is those who are tormented for being Christians who will inherit the kingdom of heaven.

5) (Matthew 5:12) the prophets.

7) The Book of Acts.

8) b) New Testament, following the Gospel of John. (Note: This makes sense since the events described in Acts take place soon after Jesus' Resurrection.)

9) (Acts 6:8) False.

10) Blasphemy is taking the Lord's name in vain. This violates the first of the Ten Commandments. When we take the Lord's name in vain, that means we are using it disrespectfully and thoughtlessly. When we use the Lord's name, it should be during worship services, to praise Him or to speak to Him in prayer.

12) (Acts 6:11) a) blasphemy. (Because the Jewish people revere the Old Testament patriarchs [such as Moses and Abraham], using their names in a disrespectful manner was considered blasphemous.)

13) (Acts 6:11) False. Stephen's enemies could not defeat his wisdom in open debate, so they convinced some men to lie about Stephen.

14) (Acts 6:15) c) an angel.

15) (Acts 7:1–53) d) by giving a speech in defense of Christianity.

16) (Acts 7:51–53) False. Stephen was saying that Israel was not faithful to the Lord, even though they were His chosen people.

17) (Acts 7:56) c) the glory of God and Jesus at God's right hand in heaven.

18) (Acts 7:56) Because he told everyone what he saw.

19) (Acts 7:57–58) a) angry.

20) (Acts 7:60) True.

22) (Acts 7:58) No.

23) (Acts 8:3) c) putting Christians in prison.

24) True.

25) (Luke 23:34) Stephen was following Jesus' example of asking God to forgive those who crucified Him. Think about the last time someone did something wrong against you. Was it hard to forgive that person? The next time you need to forgive someone, think about these examples of forgiveness.

THE EPHESIANS RECEIVE A LETTER

1) An epistle is a letter.

2) a) one of Jesus' apostles. Although Paul was an apostle of Jesus, he was not one of the original twelve disciples. Like a disciple, an apostle is a follower.

3) (Acts 8:1) False. Paul persecuted early Christians before becoming a Christian himself.

4) c) members of the church at Ephesus.

6) (Ephesians 1:1) Although many Bibles title this book "Paul's Letter to the Ephesians," Paul himself tells us he wrote the letter in the first verse.

7) (Ephesians 3:8) False.

8) (Ephesians 3:6) c) Gentiles and Jews are equal. Christ died for all who love Him, not just for one certain group of people.

9) (Ephesians 4:6) True.

10) d) Christians.

11) Be honest with each other, but in a kind way, never trying to hurt each other's feelings.

SUPER BIBLE ACTIVITIES FOR KIDS!

Barbour's Super Bible Activity Books, packed with fun illustrations and kid-friendly text, will appeal to children ages six to twelve. And the price—only $1.39—will appeal to parents. All books are paperbound. The unique size (4⅛" x 5⅜") makes these books easy to take anywhere!

A Great Selection to Satisfy All Kids!

Bible Activities
Bible Activities for Kids
Bible Connect the Dots
Bible Crosswords for Kids
Bible Picture Fun
Bible Word Games
Bible Word Searches for Kids
Clean Jokes for Kids
Fun Bible Trivia

Fun Bible Trivia 2
Great Bible Trivia for Kids
More Bible Activities
More Bible Crosswords for Kids
More Clean Jokes for Kids
Super Bible Activities
Super Bible Crosswords
Super Bible Word Searches
Super Silly Stories

Available wherever books are sold.
Or order from: Barbour Publishing, Inc.
P.O. Box 719
Uhrichsville, Ohio 44683
www.barbourbooks.com

If ordering by mail,
please include $1.00 for postage and handling per order.
Prices subject to change without notice.